THE AUSTRALIAN VERANDAH

THE

AUSTRALIAN VERANDAH

Photographs by Douglass Baglin

Text by Peter Moffitt

SUMMIT BOOKS
Published by Paul Hamlyn Pty Limited
Sydney · Auckland · London · New York

BALLARAT, VICTORIA. ADAM LINDSAY GORDON'S HOUSE

half title page: "ST MALO", HUNTERS HILL, SYDNEY
This fine house stood near the Lane Cove River and was built by Jules Joubert, the first mayor of Hunters Hill. Its verandah is of particular interest as the columns, now somewhat shortened, were taken from Burdekin House which once stood at the top of Martin Place in the city of Sydney. St Malo, by a tragedy of muddle-headed bureaucratic priorities, was demolished in 1961 to make way for an expressway.

title page: NORMANTON, NORTH QUEENSLAND
The wide verandahs in this isolated town near the Gulf of Carpentaria give precious shade in a climate which is fiercely hot all year round and very dry except for the summer monsoon season. The centre building houses the Carpentaria Shire Council. A high bauxite content in the soil gives the streets this characteristic red colour.

above: BALLARAT, VICTORIA. ADAM LINDSAY GORDON'S HOUSE
This great Australian poet was born in 1833 and died in 1870. His poetry, some of it written in this simple house where he lived in his later years, earned him a tomb in Poets' Corner of Westminister Abbey, London. His unhappy life ended when he shot himself following his daughter's death.

Summit Books
Published 1978 by Paul Hamlyn Pty Limited
176 South Creek Road, Dee Why West, NSW, Australia 2099
First published 1976
by Ure Smith, Sydney
2nd impression (limp) 1978
© Copyright Douglass Baglin (photographs),
Ure Smith (text) 1976
Designed by Gary Baulman
Produced in Australia by the Publisher
Typeset in Australia by G.T. Setters Pty Ltd.
Printed by Toppan Printing Co. (Singapore) (Pte) Limited
38 Lui Fang Road, Jurong, Singapore 22.

National Library of Australia Cataloguing-in-Publication Data

Baglin, Douglass
The Australian verandah.

First published, Sydney: Ure Smith, 1976.
ISBN 0 7271 0318 0

(1) Verandahs — Australia — Pictorial works.
I. Moffitt, Peter. II. Title.

720.8'0094

The verandah is perhaps the outstanding contribution to the distinctive architecture of Australia in the nineteenth century.

The climate and landscape of the Australian continent have great contrasts from the tropical north to the temperate south, from the green seaboard to the desert interior. Locally available building materials differ from region to region. Economic prosperity has fluctuated in time and differed from place to place. Aspirations have differed according to each person's circumstances and needs. Within such a variety of influences the verandah has evolved with a diversity of character which has become a rich part of Australia's heritage. Simple or ornate, modest or imposing, utilitarian or decorative, it is always an honest expression of the land, its climate and its people.

The early architecture of the Australian colonies was derived from the style which was familiar to the early settlers coming from England. They adapted a simplified form of the English style and built in whatever local materials were available to them. And they reacted to the harsh and inhospitable climate which was in such contrast to their homeland.

The Georgian style had already flourished for a century in England when the colony of New South Wales was first settled in 1788. It was natural that the basic form of this style, a simple geometric box with no projecting eaves, characterized the earliest Australian buildings.

Verandahs were not used in England at that time. In fact it is believed that their first use in England was in the Royal Pavilion at Brighton in 1801. But whereas the simple Georgian building was appropriate in the cool temperate climate of England, it gave poor comfort in the harsh heat of the Australian sun.

There were officers in Sydney in the first year of settlement who had served in other British Colonies where verandahs were common and were therefore aware of the virtues of a verandah in giving protection from sun and rain. It is not surprising then that verandahs appeared in Sydney at a very early stage. One of the earliest pictures of Sydney in the Watling Collection shows a verandah built along the full 22 metre frontage of the stone house built by Lieutenant-Governor Robert Ross in 1788. Ross had served with the Marines in the West Indies, the Mediterranean and North America.

It is widely believed that the verandah, and the word itself, are of Indian origin, but Robert Irving, the Australian historian, writes: "The Spanish word 'varanda' is even older than the Indian; its Portuguese meaning is given in a 16th century lexicon as 'railes to leane the brest on'. The earliest known use of the English word — in 1711 — described an Indian building.

"The verandah was indigenous to the Medieval vernacular architecture of Spain and Northern Portugal. Iberian colonists took it to Brazil, the West Indies and the coastal settlements of India. Verandahs can be seen in drawings done in Brazil, for instance, before the end of the 17th century. Later colonists in these three areas, noting the verandah's virtues in heat, humidity and heavy rain, copied it. The British imported it from the West Indies into the Northern American colonies, and Anglicized it in India. The Dutch colonists brought it to South Africa. The British military builders played an important part in this spread as they were posted from garrison to garrison, and the early introduction of the verandah into Australia was inevitable."

As architectural fashions changed in Australia the style of verandahs went through a continuing evolution. Until the First World War the styles followed fairly closely what was happening in England and they are commonly known by the name of the monarch of the time.

Fashions changed more slowly in the earlier days of Australia's history than they do now. The Colonial Georgian style persisted here for some sixty years until about 1850. Buildings were usually symmetrical and followed well under-

EXPERIMENT FARM COTTAGE, PARRAMATTA, NEW SOUTH WALES

MACQUARIE FIELDS HOUSE, MACQUARIE FIELDS, NEW SOUTH WALES

This late Georgian house has a verandah of great elegance. It was very probably designed for John Hosking, the first Mayor of Sydney, and dates from approximately 1843. The verandah columns are turned timber. This house very clearly illustrates the strict symmetry and simple lines of the Georgian style. It is a clear example of the Australian addition of a verandah to a simple Georgian box.

EXPERIMENT FARM COTTAGE, PARRAMATTA, NEW SOUTH WALES

Built by Surgeon John Harris some time before 1821 on the site of James Ruse's "Experiment Farm". This name was given by Governor Phillip when he installed the ex-convict Ruse on a two-acre plot "in order to know in what time a man might be able to cultivate a sufficient quantity of ground to support himself". Ruse became the first settler in Australia to harvest wheat and when in 1791 he assured the Governor that the experiment could be regarded as a success he was given 30 acres as a grant on which to continue his farming. This was the first land grant in Australia. The cottage is a fine example of small Colonial Georgian style — symmetrical, simple and elegant. It was acquired in 1961 by the National Trust and restored.

MACQUARIE FIELDS HOUSE, MACQUARIE FIELDS, NEW SOUTH WALES

"COMO", MELBOURNE

Built in 1850 by Edward Eyre Williams, "Como" is one of Melbourne's finest houses. Its verandahs are well proportioned and elegant. The iron spear balustrades have rods of wrought iron with cast iron spear heads. This early Victorian simplicity contrasts greatly with the "wedding cake" complexity of late Victorian ironwork.

RETFORD PARK, BOWRAL, NEW SOUTH WALES

This fine example of a mansion of the late Victorian period was the country home of Anthony Hordern whose retail department store in George Street, Sydney, on Brickfield Hill was famous for many years. The entrance portico and tower show an influence of the Italianate style.

PAGES 10–11
PRESBYTERIAN BOYS' HOME, LEPPINGTON, NEW SOUTH WALES

The old timber farmhouse was converted as principal's residence and administrative office when the Boys' Home at Leppington was built in 1962. The new building, an excellent example of the modern use of verandahs, was designed by Ian McKay and Philip Cox and won the Sulman Award, the highest award for architecture in New South Wales.

"COMO", MELBOURNE

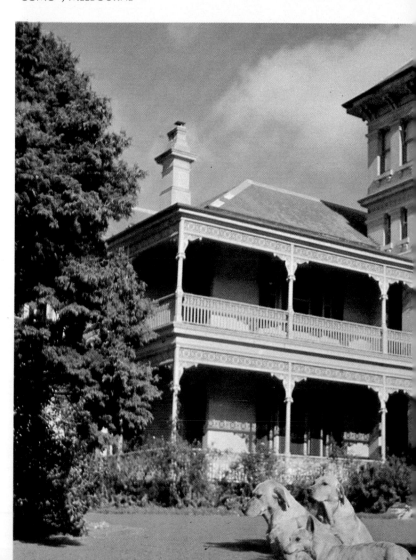

RETFORD PARK, BOWRAL,
NEW SOUTH WALES

stood rules of design. Decorative detail was simple and verandahs were built usually of timber with shingled roofs.

The vast majority of Colonial Georgian buildings in Australia are to be found in New South Wales and Tasmania. These two States were the earliest to be settled and by the time the other States were settled the style was changing, or had completely changed, in favour of the Victorian style.

Although Queen Victoria's rule commenced in 1837, the style which bears her name did not filter through to Australia until about 1850. The Victorian style broke away from strict rules of design and developed with a far greater variety. Buildings became less symmetrical and their verandahs, in particular, were characterized by the abundant use of highly decorative cast iron "lace". As a result of the Industrial Revolution iron was now a cheap material. It could be cast into an infinite variety of intricate patterns and was widely used for balustrade and frieze panels and supporting columns.

During the 40 years between 1850 and 1890 the economic wealth of the gold mining boom resulted in a frenzied era of building. The virtues of verandahs and balconies were well understood and the verandah had become an integral part of the Australian vernacular tradition.

The boom burst in 1893 and during the resulting depression, until the turn of the century, very little building took place. By the time building activity started to move again the style had changed. The Federation period saw a continuation of the verandah tradition until the First World War but decoration showed a reaction against the "wedding cake" fussiness of the earlier Victorian period. In place of cast iron lace, decorative patterns were cut in timber. The timber decoration of verandahs is shown nowhere better than the unique Queensland domestic style. Decorative style was influenced during this time by the Arts and Crafts movement of Europe and the use of motifs from nature in the Art Nouveau movement.

In the period between the two World Wars the verandah tradition languished under the influence of imported styles. The "Canadian Bungalow" influence produced in Australia what Robin Boyd described with no affection as the "triple-fronted bung", and verandahs had shrunk to porches. Australians had turned their backs on something of value in favour of fickle fashion. The vernacular style house lost its graceful and functional verandah and became a barefaced box unsuited to the climate. Worse still, this arid style of the suburban sprawl spread to country towns and country homesteads, and the singularly most valuable aspect of what had been developing as an appropriate Australian style lost popularity.

In the last ten or fifteen years Australians have started to turn again in recognition of the verandah, led by a vanguard of clear minded architects who are not hidebound by the fashionable dictates of European and American styles. It is heartening to see so many Australians looking again at our past and recognizing that we developed something valuable which combined utility with grace, something which is every bit as valid today as it was a century ago.

The climate of most regions of Australia is rigorous and changeable. The verandah is an exceptionally practical device, sheltering people from sun and rain, shielding the walls of the building from the heat of the sun and contributing much to its coolness in hot weather. Verandahs and balconies provide additional cool living and sleeping areas, catching the slightest breeze on summer evenings, when buildings of brick or stone during long hot periods remain reservoirs of heat well into the night. The real comfort of these outdoor living areas, and the benefit of shielding the walls and windows from the summer sun, is well known and is being increasingly recognized in the design of modern buildings based on scientific principles. And in areas of low rainfall the extra roof area catches additional rain for precious drinking water.

Yet despite these virtues of utility Australians descended into a period of verandah hatred. Popular opinion often fails to recognize the value of our old buildings. Fashions today change rapidly and the artistic values of a fairly recent past are commonly despised or under-rated. The street verandahs of our country towns, one of the few things recognized abroad as being distinctively and characteristically Australian, suffered this fate. Joe Glascott, writing in the *Sydney Morning Herald* on 4 January 1969, said: "It is hard to pin down exactly what started the great verandah hatred. But we know that in the 1940s aldermen and councillors throughout New South Wales decided to modernize their towns.

"Modernize to councillors unfortunately usually means to destroy. So out came the axes and down came the main street verandah posts and overhead balconies in town after town throughout the State.

"The verandah posts which gave towns and rural cities their character and individuality, and the balconies with their delicate cast-iron balustrades which gave them a unique Australian-ness, were stripped from the main street buildings in an orgy of modernizing.

"Now that most of the New South Wales towns have achieved this aim they have become copies of metropolitan suburbia. . .

GULGONG, NEW SOUTH WALES

"Many old verandahs and balconies have been replaced by stark steel cantilevered awnings. In other cases they have been left denuded like aged aunts in mini-skirts."

We should not aim at keeping everything that is old simply because it is old, but we must be careful in preserving what is good from our past and what can be used well. Professor J. Burke of the University of Melbourne, addressing a seminar in Canberra on historic preservation, said: "The challenge to the imaginative planner is that modern industries, cities and townships should expand and proliferate in a setting which preserves the beauty of nature and the heritage of history. Conservation does not mean conservatism. It is an abuse of history to wrap ourselves up in dreams of the past, but no nation has become great by rejecting its past or neglecting to honour it. One of the questions which posterity will ask about this generation is how it has discharged its obligation to preserve the national heritage."

One of the most significant and most visible aspects of our national heritage, one which contributes so much of value to the streetscape of our towns and cities, is the Australian verandah.

GULGONG, NEW SOUTH WALES

Gulgong, the gold mining town "on the Ten Dollar note", is worthy of such distinction for its careful preservation of street verandahs with their verandah posts. This town has found great reward and acclaim from its tourist trade, attracted almost solely by the streetscape which has not been blindly destroyed in the name of "progress". Gulgong may not be rich as a centre of commerce but in terms of its architectural streetscape it is one of the richest towns in Australia. Its citizens and their local council are showing great wisdom by restoring old footpath verandahs in need of repair and in some cases replacing them, complete with verandah posts, where they have been removed in the past.

The people of Gulgong are very much aware of their valuable architectural heritage. They are restoring their street verandahs rather than pulling them down.

QUEEN STREET, CAMPBELLTOWN, NEW SOUTH WALES

Three stages in the saga of an 1840s building in the main street of historic Campbelltown. The first photograph shows the old building in a state of disrepair but still alive and in use. The second photograph shows it empty, abandoned and stripped by vandals—a sad and demoralizing sight. The building was then proclaimed a historic building under the County of Cumberland Planning Scheme, along with two neighbouring buildings to the left and one to the right. It was acquired by the New South Wales Planning and Environment Commission and restored by them with the assistance of architect Morton Herman. The third photograph shows the building in use again after restoration, once again a proud building. This is an excellent example of the fact that an old building which on the surface may appear to many people to be beyond salvation can be restored at less cost than demolition and reconstruction. Not only can we save money but we can also save our own national soul, and our heritage.

VICTORIA BARRACKS, PADDINGTON, SYDNEY

Designed by Major George Barney commanding the Royal Engineers, Victoria Barracks, named of course after Queen Victoria, was begun in 1841 and took seven years to build. The stone was quarried on the spot and the work was carried out by convicts under the supervision of the Royal Engineers. The long verandah has an iron structure and an iron balustrade. The Army is to be commended for its active interest in recent years in the restoration and preservation of the finest old army barracks in Australia.

TULLY, CENTRAL COAST,
QUEENSLAND
The town has an extremely high rainfall
and is surrounded by tropical
rainforest. Most of the verandahs of the
street were intact when this photograph
was taken in 1967. They provide
excellent shelter. The washing is drying
on the verandah of the historic Tully
Hotel.

TWOFOLD BAY, NEW SOUTH WALES
"Edrom" with its huge verandah was
built in 1914 by the Monaro grazier
John Logan. Like Ben Boyd the whaler
he had a vision of spectacular
development at Twofold Bay but he
ended in financial ruin.

POST OFFICE, BROKEN HILL, NEW
SOUTH WALES
The "Silver City" in far western New
South Wales began as a frontier mining
town when Charles Rasp, a boundary
rider, discovered one of the richest
silver-lead-zinc deposits in the world.
The verandah gives valuable shade in
the street of this remote city in one of
Australia's hottest areas where
temperatures soar over 100° F for days
on end.

TULLY, CENTRAL COAST, QUEENSLAND

TWOFOLD BAY, NEW SOUTH WALES

MOLONG, NEW SOUTH WALES
The Yarn Market Cottage, Molong,
was built in 1860. It was restored by
the Yarn Market Association in 1972
and now functions as a Craft Cottage.

"CLIFTON", HUNTERS HILL, SYDNEY
One of the best and most highly
decorated iron verandahs in Sydney.
Note that the decorative balustrade and
frieze panels are wrought iron rather
than cast iron. The columns are cast
iron. Set in an extensive and beautiful
garden, it has excellent views of the
Parramatta River. With verandahs facing
all points of the compass it is generally
possible to find a lee side in the worst of
weather.

KAPUNDA, SOUTH AUSTRALIA
South Australia has a distinctive
regional style in the use of bluestone
for walls in heavy contrast with the light
delicacy of the cast iron columns and
lace decoration of the verandah. This
example in Kapunda, dating from the
late Victorian period, typifies this
regional style.

"CLIFTON", HUNTERS HILL, SYDNEY

WALDHEIM CHALET, TASMANIA

"BAROONA", SINGLETON, NEW SOUTH WALES

This is one of the finest homesteads in the Hunter Valley, built by the pioneer Dangar family. Its wide verandah has paving of stone slabs and a very unusual character of roof with curved beams and heavy Doric columns.

WALDHEIM CHALET, TASMANIA

Built in the Alps of Tasmania in 1912 by the Austrian Gustav Weindorfer who loved solitude and native animals. The timber posts and shingles show something of an Austrian influence translated through readily available local materials.

McGUIRE'S HUT, BEN HALL SERIES, MEGALONG VALLEY, NEW SOUTH WALES

The "Ben Hall" television series was filmed on Douglass Baglin's property in the Megalong Valley of the Blue Mountains. The huts were built by the makers of the film as faithful reproductions of early settlers' huts of the period. This hut has a bark roof but the verandah is roofed with tea tree brush which is not rainproof but provides shade from the sun.

McGUIRE'S HUT, NEW SOUTH WALES

23

ARMIDALE, NEW SOUTH WALES
The verandahs are an essential part of the life of the country towns and cities. Hotel verandahs provide excellent summer sleep-outs. This hotel verandah in Armidale on the New England tablelands of northern New South Wales is a good vantage point for people watching the Anzac Day procession. Note the barber's poles in the foreground.

SEPPELTSFIELD, BAROSSA VALLEY, SOUTH AUSTRALIA

SEPPELTSFIELD, BAROSSA VALLEY, SOUTH AUSTRALIA
The wine-making industry of the Barossa Valley evolved through the efforts of a Scot, George Fife Angus, and German winemakers led by Johann Gramp. Later the Seppelt family built this cellar building of bluestone with its elegant verandahs which provide shade and help to keep the building cool.

CHINATOWN, BROOME, WESTERN AUSTRALIA
The galvanized iron verandahs are characteristic of Broome in north-western Australia, a town famous for its pearling industry. These shops and houses are peopled by a multi-racial society of Malays-Chinese-Europeans-Aborigines.

CHINATOWN, BROOME, WESTERN AUSTRALIA

THE PARSONAGE, CASSILIS, NEW SOUTH WALES

ST ALBANS, NEW SOUTH WALES

THE PARSONAGE, CASSILIS, NEW
SOUTH WALES
This simple colonial Georgian cottage is
the parsonage for the Anglican Church
at Cassilis, a tiny pocket of fine early
sandstone buildings in the Hunter
Valley. The verandah completely
surrounds the house and is typical of
early homesteads of the area.

ST ALBANS, NEW SOUTH WALES
This old cottage of Mat Thompson the
stockman has a verandah of simple
construction using timber poles, readily
available local materials, for the roof
rafters. The verandah beams have been
roughly squared with an adze. Everyday
gear is hung on pegs on the wall.

THE DOCTOR'S HOUSE, WINDSOR,
NEW SOUTH WALES
Built in the 1830s as a house and inn,
this was one of the earliest buildings of
Windsor and overlooks the
Hawkesbury River. The balcony was not
originally roofed and the ironwork is of
a slightly later date. The house was
more recently occupied for many years
by doctors, hence its name.

THE DOCTOR'S HOUSE, WINDSOR,
NEW SOUTH WALES

LINESMEN'S QUARTERS, CENTRAL AUSTRALIA

LINESMEN'S QUARTERS, CENTRAL AUSTRALIA

The railway line and overland telegraph line from Adelaide to Alice Springs run across the desert heart of Australia. This building stands alongside the railway line and accommodates maintenance workmen who use the shower in the wooden log structure under the tank for bathing. The house is completely surrounded by a verandah to combat the intense heat of the desert.

SILVERTON, NEW SOUTH WALES

The Municipal Chambers at Silverton, one of the few remaining buildings in what was once a thriving mining town close to Broken Hill in far western New South Wales.

MOSS VALE, NEW SOUTH WALES

Barnsley's corner store at Moss Vale sells "everything" as the sign says. The verandah roof has bull-nosed iron and is supported by iron brackets.

MOSS VALE, NEW SOUTH WALES

SILVERTON, NEW SOUTH WALES

BROOME, WESTERN AUSTRALIA

HUNTERS HILL, SYDNEY
This verandah from the late Victorian period has a curious tower-like structure on the corner which has some suggestion of Islamic influence and is a good example of the Romantic excesses which were not uncommon in this period.

BROOME, WESTERN AUSTRALIA
The Post Office at Broome on the north-western coast of Australia is highly characteristic of vernacular buildings which have evolved to suit the climate. Broome is intensely hot all year and during the monsoon season extremely humid. This building is designed to take advantage of the cooling effects of natural ventilation in a hot humid climate and its verandahs are an essential element. They shade the walls and allow the doors and windows to remain open even during heavy rain.

OBERON, NEW SOUTH WALES
The verandah surrounding this simple sheep station homestead gives it protection in the extremes of climate from winter snow and rain to scorching summer sun.

OBERON, NEW SOUTH WALES

POST OFFICE & COURT HOUSE,
BATHURST, NEW SOUTH WALES
Designed by James Barnet and
completed in 1880, this important
group of public buildings in the historic
city of Bathurst have fine verandahs
which are both noble in character and
highly utilitarian.

LAUNCESTON, TASMANIA
The verandah of this magnificent
mansion makes a great contribution to
its grace and elegance.

CUE, WESTERN AUSTRALIA
A hot little miner's hut in this isolated
old mining town would be even hotter
without the shade from its small
verandah.

POST OFFICE & COURT HOUSE, BATHURST, NEW SOUTH WALES

LAUNCESTON, TASMANIA

CUE, WESTERN AUSTRALIA

KURUMBA STATION, QUEENSLAND

ANDAMOOKA, SOUTH AUSTRALIA

KURUMBA STATION, QUEENSLAND
This homestead in the Gulf Country of
Queensland is elevated on stilts for air
circulation underneath and to provide
useful sheltered space under the house.
The verandah has glass louvres to keep
out the heavy summer monsoon rains.

ANDAMOOKA, SOUTH AUSTRALIA
The verandah on this opal miner's hut is
made of grass bound together with
wire. There are very few building
timbers in this bare, arid area. The hut
tells its own story of hardship.

NORMANTON, QUEENSLAND
The Carpentaria Shire Council Building
stands in proud isolation in streets of
red earth. The infill of timber boards,
scalloped at the bottom, under the
upper verandah is characteristic of
many Queensland buildings of this
period.

NORMANTON, QUEENSLAND

HUNTERS HILL, SYDNEY

HUNTERS HILL, SYDNEY
Verandahs add grace and style to living
in many fine old sandstone homes in
Hunters Hill.

DERBY, WESTERN AUSTRALIA
This hut, standing near an old Baobab
tree, has been supplied by the
government for housing of Aborigines,
who much prefer being outside in the
shade of the verandah.

HAY, NEW SOUTH WALES

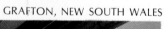

GRAFTON, NEW SOUTH WALES

"LANGAWIRRA" STATION, NEW SOUTH WALES

HAY, NEW SOUTH WALES
This footpath verandah in Hay in western New South Wales provides shade from the hot sun and is a popular meeting place. Verandahs like this give towns a personality which delights visitors, particularly those from overseas who are aware of the uniqueness of the Australian footpath verandah.

GRAFTON, NEW SOUTH WALES
The verandah of the Grafton Bowling Club overlooks the Clarence River and is an excellent place to have a cold beer on a hot day. The verandah is elevated to escape the frequent floods.

"LANGAWIRRA" STATION, NEW SOUTH WALES
Adzed posts and simple round tree poles covered with galvanized iron make the verandah of Langawirra homestead — a huge sheep station 75 miles from Broken Hill. John Gall, son of the owner, waters the pot plants. A squatter's chair is in the foreground.

ARMIDALE, NEW SOUTH WALES
At Armidale on the New England table-lands, a crowd waits on the verandah of the Folk Museum for its doors to open. Built in 1915, the use of cast iron verandah decoration was not typical of the period but shows that in any transition from one style to the next there has always been a period of overlap.

ARMIDALE, NEW SOUTH WALES

WYNDHAM, WESTERN AUSTRALIA

The verandah of the Hotel Wyndham in the main street of one of the hottest towns in this country.

LITHGOW, NEW SOUTH WALES

Esbank House in Lithgow at the western foot of the Blue Mountains, 150 kilometres from Sydney, has a simple verandah surrounding its stone walls. The symmetry of the Colonial Georgian Style is evident with the front door on the central axis and with two front windows and two chimneys symmetrically placed either side. Without the shade of the verandah the stone walls would heat up in the summer sun and retain their heat long into the night, making sleeping conditions very uncomfortable.

BUNDABERG, QUEENSLAND

Queensland has its own distinctive style of verandah. This friendly family home in Bundaberg reflects the good taste of tropical life in a region with a wonderful climate. The verandah is one of the main activity areas. This one has timber posts and rails and decoration of cast iron. The slatted timber infill to the space under the verandah floor is typical of the Queensland style. Note the walls of this house: the timber framing is lined on the inside only.

WYNDHAM, WESTERN AUSTRALIA

LITHGOW, NEW SOUTH WALES

BUNDABERG, QUEENSLAND

"ST MALO", HUNTERS HILL, SYDNEY
Looking along the verandah of St Malo
with its black and white marble floor
tiles. The National Trust and many other
groups and individuals waged a bitter
struggle for two years in the 1960s when
the Department of Main Roads wanted
the building demolished for an
expressway. Even though it was possible
to slightly change the route of the
expressway to save the building,
bureaucracy eventually won the battle
and it must be to the everlasting shame
of Sydney that such a treasure was lost.

TRUNKEY, NEW SOUTH WALES
Carved timber brackets add a small
touch of decoration to the verandah of
Fred Davies' corner shop at Trunkey
near Bathurst.

"ST MALO",
HUNTERS HILL,
SYDNEY

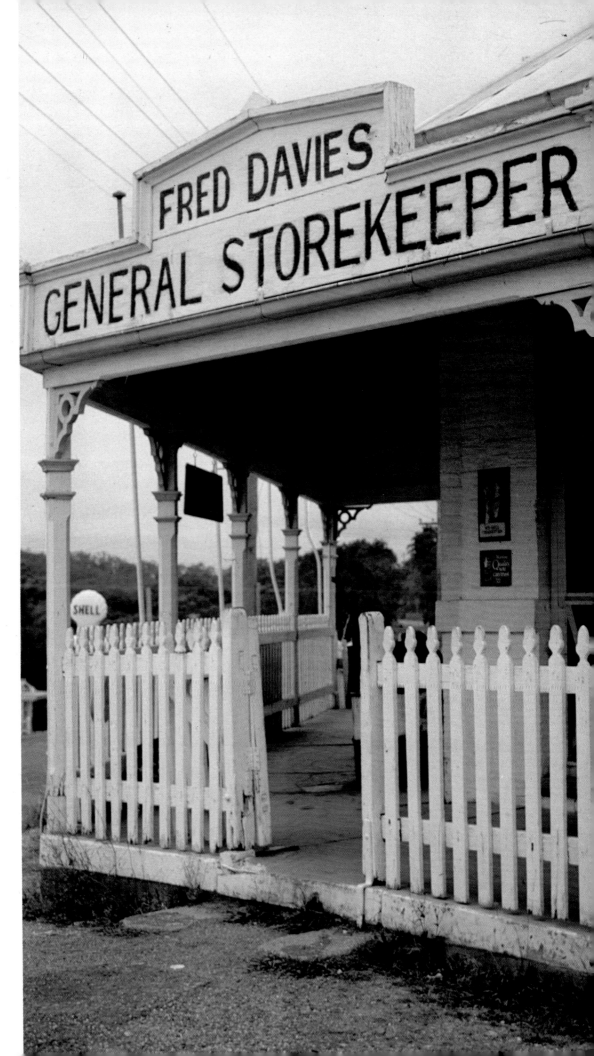

FRED DAVIES
GENERAL STOREKEEPER

SHELL

MEEKATHARRA, WESTERN AUSTRALIA

DARLING POINT, SYDNEY
At one time, not so long ago, Darling
Point had far more fine old buildings
like this one, but many have been
demolished to make way for multi-
storey home unit buildings. The french
doors open on to a wide verandah and
have timber shutters for privacy and
ventilation. The verandah ironwork is
particularly delicate.

MEEKATHARRA, WESTERN
AUSTRALIA
This hotel was built about 1890 when
Meekatharra was a prosperous gold
mining town. Many towns like this one
thrived during a period of gold mining
activity but almost died when the ore
ran out.

BATHURST, NEW SOUTH WALES
The railway station built at Bathurst in
1876 shows a Dutch influence of style in
the shape of its gable ends. Its verandah
frieze decoration is of carved timber
with motifs of Gothic origin — strange
ingredients to find in an otherwise
ordinary Australian country town
building of the Victorian period.

BATHURST, NEW SOUTH WALES

HILL END, NEW SOUTH WALES
Pioneer's hut on the goldfields of Hill
End near Mudgee. Hill End flourished
in the gold rush of the 1850s.

MINORE, NEW SOUTH WALES

WATSONS BAY, SYDNEY

MONA VALE, SYDNEY

MINORE, NEW SOUTH WALES
The old Post Office of Minore near Dubbo, a plain little timber building except for the scalloped bargeboard and the serrated fringe on the bull-nosed iron verandah.

WATSONS BAY, SYDNEY
The simple verandah of the old "Ozone" fish restaurant on the harbourside beach of Watsons Bay shades one of the most delightful outdoor eating spots in Sydney. Now operated by the Doyle family, it is known as "Doyle's On the Beach" and is famous for its superb seafoods.

MONA VALE, SYDNEY
The strange mixture of styles gives this house and verandah its idiosyncrasy, which is heightened by the deluded grandeur of its circular entrance pathway.

RANDWICK, SYDNEY
The extensive verandah of the Royal Hotel at Randwick is thankfully intact as it is one of the very best remaining examples of hotel verandah ironwork of the Victorian period in Australia.

RANDWICK, SYDNEY

51

BELL, NEW SOUTH WALES
The verandah of Holly Lodge at Bell in the Blue Mountains gives winter snow protection to the house.

"FERNHILL", MULGOA, SYDNEY
Built in 1840 by Edward Cox, son of Captain William Cox who built the first road over the Blue Mountains, this Colonial Georgian house is notable for the neo-Greek influence in its curved verandah or loggia and its Greek Doric sandstone columns.

BELL, NEW SOUTH WALES

MILDURA, VICTORIA

The timber decoration of this verandah is remarkably delicate and intricate and is given a feeling of lightness by its slender turned timber posts. The house was built by the Chaffey brothers, Canadian irrigation engineers who settled in Mildura in 1866 and began what is now a major irrigation project taking water from the Murray River to what was once arid wasteland. In context of the period, this verandah is unusual in that the upper deck has no roof, but this was quite common in North America at the time.

URALLA, NEW SOUTH WALES

The verandah of this early timber house at Uralla catches an essential supply of drinking water.

IPSWICH, QUEENSLAND

This characteristic Queensland building, "Osanam House", has a verandah of intricate timber decoration. As in many other cases it is interesting to imagine what the house would look like if the verandah did not exist.

URALLA, NEW SOUTH WALES

54

IPSWICH, QUEENSLAND
Another Queensland delight is the famous Ipswich Club with its verandah intricately decorated in timberwork in characteristic Queensland idiom.

SWAN HILL, VICTORIA
A verandah post painted as a barber's pole proclaims the use of this building at the Swan Hill Museum. The building dates from about 1880.

"GUNTAWANG", GULGONG, NEW SOUTH WALES
Built about 1865 as the homestead of a grazing property and horse stud. The verandah has open work iron posts and carved timber frieze.

IPSWICH, QUEENSLAND

"GUNTAWANG",
GULGONG, NEW SOUTH WALES

MOLONG, NEW SOUTH WALES

MOLONG, NEW SOUTH WALES
Built before 1879, this building has had
a varied history. It has been
successively a general store, a stock
and station agency, a refreshment
room and boarding house, and a
grocery and ironmongery store before
becoming the office of the *Molong
Express* newspaper. The *Express* was
published here from 1929 until 1978
when it moved its premises to the
opposite side of the street.

CARCOAR, NEW SOUTH WALES
Another unique town with its street
verandahs intact and most of them well
kept.

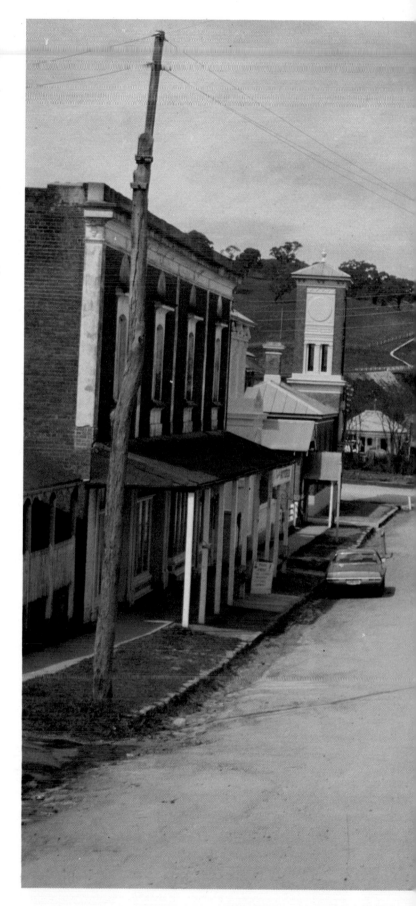

CARCOAR, NEW SOUTH WALES

DARWIN, NORTHERN TERRITORY

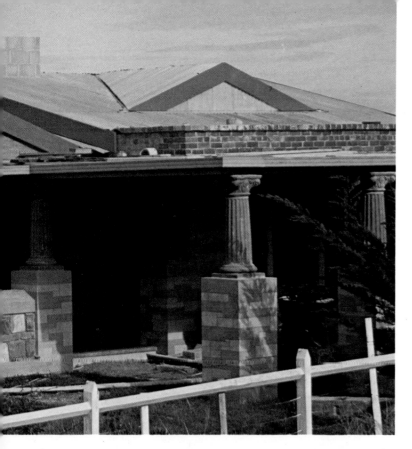

KANGAROO ISLAND, SOUTH AUSTRALIA

A verandah of heavy construction on a windswept island in Spencer Gulf. Flinders named the island because of large mobs of kangaroos he noticed during his visit there in 1802.

DARWIN, NORTHERN TERRITORY

The original Roman Catholic Church at Darwin was a building with great historic association. It was destroyed by Cyclone Tracy at Christmas 1974, when much of Darwin was devastated and many lives were lost.

HURSTVILLE, SYDNEY

This fine old home of the late Victorian period has a wonderful example of cast iron "lace" on its verandahs.

KANGAROO ISLAND,
SOUTH AUSTRALIA

HURSTVILLE, SYDNEY

COOKTOWN, QUEENSLAND
Galvanized iron is used a great deal for the cladding of buildings in remote towns of Queensland. This building has great rustic charm. Now virtually a ghost town, Cooktown, situated on the Endeavour River, was once a thriving port: in 1874 it had 94 hotels in its main street which was two miles long.

TIBOOBURRA, NEW SOUTH WALES
The shade from this verandah speaks for itself. Tibooburra is a remote pastoral frontier town in hot, arid, far western New South Wales.

"INVERARY PARK", BUNGONIA, NEW SOUTH WALES
Built in the 1830s by Dr David Reid who came to Australia as Surgeon-Superintendent of convict ships. The house has random stone rubble walls 600 mm thick covered with stucco. Its steeply pitched roof, containing attic bedrooms, spreads out over the verandah and is supported by timber verandah columns. It is the prototype of the early Australian country house with attics.

COOKTOWN, QUEENSLAND

"INVERARY PARK",
BUNGONIA, NEW SOUTH WALES

TIBOOBURRA, NEW SOUTH WALES

HORSLEY, SYDNEY

This steeply-roofed verandah is on a small out-building of the famous 'Horsley' homestead near Parramatta which has the intriguing address of 'Horsley', Horsley Road, Horsley. Built by the Weston family in 1831, it was occupied by the same family for a century. In the 1930s the property and homestead were bought by the Moffitt family who occupied it for almost 40 years.

HUNTERS HILL, SYDNEY

HUNTERS HILL, SYDNEY
"Vienna", another of the houses built
by the Joubert brothers, has further
variations on the theme of carved
timber verandah decoration.

MURRELLA PARK STATION,
NORTHERN TERRITORY
The verandah roof of this hut is of paper
bark (*Melaleuca*); the timber poles
which form the walls and verandah
posts are from the screw palm or
Pandanus.

"WOODSTONE", BATHURST, NEW
SOUTH WALES
The verandahs of this house of the late
Victorian period are a good example of
the use of cast iron verandah posts and
intricately patterned cast iron "lace"
for the balustrade and frieze panels.

MURRELLA PARK STATION,
NORTHERN TERRITORY

BUTCHER'S HUT, "KURRAJONG PARK", CASSILIS, NEW SOUTH WALES
Meat killed on the property was hung in this outbuilding. The hardwood of the simple slab hut has turned a beautiful grey with exposure to the weather.

COSSACK, WESTERN AUSTRALIA
An old government building at Cossack, near Roebourne in north-western Australia. This former pearling port was closed down when the fleet and much of the town was destroyed by a cyclone in 1873. Note the timber battens holding down the iron roof sheeting and the steel straps holding down the roof on to the walls.

TIBOOBURRA, NEW SOUTH WALES
A simple verandah shades the walls of Kennewells Hotel in Tibooburra, one of the hottest, driest and most remote towns in Australia.

DARWIN, NORTHERN TERRITORY
The verandah of the Administrator's residence, built in 1870, has adjustable timber shutters to control the air flow. The climate is hot all year and dry except during the monsoon season when it is very humid. This building survived Cyclone Tracy in 1974.

COSSACK, WESTERN AUSTRALIA

TIBOOBURRA,
NEW SOUTH WALES

70

DARWIN, NORTHERN TERRITORY

COSSACK, WESTERN AUSTRALIA

LAUNCESTON, TASMANIA
This old home, now used as a Wesleyan chapel, is a good example of the decorative excesses of the late Victorian period, shown here with a slight Gothic influence.

COSSACK, WESTERN AUSTRALIA
This old government building at Cossack, now deserted, survived the cyclone of 1873 which wiped out the fleet and closed down the pearling industry.

URALLA, NEW SOUTH WALES
Before the advent of the motor car, when a day's travel covered a short distance, hotels in country towns, such as this one in Uralla built in 1909, played a much more important role in accommodating travellers than they do today. Their verandahs were often used for sleeping an overflow of guests.

Behold the turtle . . .
makes progress
ly when his neck
out."

Y'S BOOKSHOP
1507 WILMOT PLACE
Around the corner from
the Oak Bay Theatre
VICTORIA, B.C.
TELEPHONE 385-2021

URALLA, NEW SOUTH WALES

CHILLAGOE, QUEENSLAND

CANBERRA, AUSTRALIAN CAPITAL TERRITORY

CHILLAGOE, QUEENSLAND
The Post Office Hotel is an oasis in remote, sweltering Cape York Peninsula where one patron has escaped the sun by parking his car in the shade of the verandah. The truck was used by Douglass Baglin to travel from Mitchell River to Cairns to beat the floods of 1967, sleeping on the mattress on top of the load.

CANBERRA, AUSTRALIAN CAPITAL TERRITORY
The verandah of this simple pioneer's timber slab house provided well-used outdoor living space.

STUART TOWN, NEW SOUTH WALES
This verandah is typical of the simple structures built in old mining towns. Stuart Town, once thriving with activity, is now almost deserted.

STUART TOWN, NEW SOUTH WALES

"LYNWOOD", GUILDFORD, SYDNEY

"YALLUNDRY" HOMESTEAD,
CUMNOCK, NEW SOUTH WALES
Built in the early years of this century,
the verandah now has flyscreens to
keep out summer insects.

"LYNWOOD", GUILDFORD, SYDNEY
This verandah from the late Victorian
period has a fine tiled floor surrounded
by an edging of white marble.

"YALLUNDRY" HOMESTEAD,
CUMNOCK, NEW SOUTH WALES

"COOMA COTTAGE", YASS, NEW SOUTH WALES

Built in 1836 by Cornelius O'Brien, this house was purchased in 1841 by Hamilton Hume, the famous explorer and pastoralist who discovered the Murray River. He lived there for more than 30 years until his death in 1873. The roof was originally of timber shingles and most of the original turned timber verandah posts have been replaced with plain posts. The verandah floor is brick paved. "Cooma Cottage" is now owned by the National Trust and is being restored.

"HOBARTVILLE", WINDSOR, NEW SOUTH WALES

One of Australia's finest Georgian country houses, "Hobartville" was built in the late 1820s by William Cox. The rear or garden façade in this photograph shows the verandah following the line of the three-sided projecting bay containing the drawing room on the ground floor and the master bedroom on the upper floor. The original turned wooden verandah columns have since been replaced by cast iron supports.

"COOMA COTTAGE", YASS, NEW SOUTH WALES

"HOBARTVILLE",
WINDSOR, NEW SOUTH WALES

OLD HOTEL AT EMERALD, QUEENSLAND

This architectural curiosity has a character which is distinctly of Queensland. It is built on timber stumps, allowing free air movement under the building. The verandah has a corrugated iron roof, timber verandah posts, a cast iron balustrade upstairs and arched infills of timber boarding below to give additional shade. The walls of the building have an exposed timber frame with lining boards on the inside only, a fairly common practice in Queensland at the time, mainly for economy. The ladder from the upstairs balcony is a regulation fire escape. It is interesting to imagine what this building would look like without its verandahs.

BARMERA, SOUTH AUSTRALIA

COOKTOWN, NORTH QUEENSLAND

BARMERA, SOUTH AUSTRALIA
Signs on the verandah of this corner
store in one of the wine-growing areas
of South Australia advertise everything
from pest extermination to Coca-Cola.

COOKTOWN, NORTH QUEENSLAND
The verandah of this old house has a
view of the Endeavour River where
Captain James Cook careened his ship
in 1770.

TOWNSVILLE, QUEENSLAND
This architectural curiosity on the north
coast of Queensland has to be seen to
be believed.

DUBBO, NEW SOUTH WALES
The romantic little verandah on this
timber cottage dates from the early
years of this century.

TOWNSVILLE, QUEENSLAND

DUBBO, NEW SOUTH WALES

PORT PIRIE, SOUTH AUSTRALIA
This town has a railway station which is
a gem of country railway station
architecture of the Victorian era.
Passengers wait in the shelter of its
verandah for the train which runs up
the middle of the main street and stops
in the roadway in front of the station.

**DALKEITH, PERTH, WESTERN
AUSTRALIA**
One wonders what sort of commanding
view there must be from the verandah
of this fine old home.

SCONE, NEW SOUTH WALES
Verandahs have many uses.

PORT PIRIE, SOUTH AUSTRALIA

DALKEITH, PERTH, WESTERN AUSTRALIA

SCONE,
NEW SOUTH WALES

DARWIN, NORTHERN TERRITORY

BROOME, WESTERN AUSTRALIA

DARWIN, NORTHERN TERRITORY
It was here that the first Japanese
bombs fell on Australian soil in 1942.
The building also survived Cyclone
Tracy in 1974.

BROOME, WESTERN AUSTRALIA
A Japanese air-raid in 1942 caught a
number of Dutch Dornier flying boats
from Indonesia moored in the bay as
they refuelled. People watched helpless
from the verandah of the Continental
Hotel as many women and children
died in the sunken aircraft.

LUDDENHAM, NEW SOUTH WALES
An abandoned pioneer's timber slab
house had its simple traditional
verandah.

LUDDENHAM,
NEW SOUTH WALES

CASTLE HILL, TOWNSVILLE, QUEENSLAND

CASTLE HILL, TOWNSVILLE, QUEENSLAND

Australia's great little corner stores give a wonderful service. This one, complete with the inevitable verandah signs, stands at the foot of towering Castle Hill.

BONDI JUNCTION, SYDNEY

The imposing verandah roof on this small cottage has all the delusions of grandeur which were common in late Victorian architecture.

BRISBANE, QUEENSLAND

Cast iron "lace" decorates the verandah of this timber house in suburban Brisbane.

BRISBANE, QUEENSLAND

PORT HEDLAND, WESTERN AUSTRALIA

KALUMBURU, WESTERN AUSTRALIA

PORT HEDLAND, WESTERN AUSTRALIA
Baobab trees shade the verandah of a pearler's home at Port Hedland.

KALUMBURU, WESTERN AUSTRALIA
The historic Spanish Roman Catholic mission has a verandah balustrade made of wire mesh used for reinforcing concrete. The walls of this remote Aboriginal mission building are covered with corrugated iron.

KALGOORLIE, WESTERN AUSTRALIA
The main street of Kalgoorlie, one of the greatest verandah towns in Western Australia, is called the "golden mile" after Paddy Hannan's discovery of the rich gold deposits in 1893. The almost unbroken line of verandahs over the footpath shade the people and shops in this hot arid town and give it wonderful charm and character and a valuable link with its past.

KALGOORLIE, WESTERN AUSTRALIA

91

"DUNTRYLEAGUE", ORANGE, NEW SOUTH WALES.
Built in 1876 as one of the largest and best country homesteads in the State, this magnificent building is now the headquarters of the Orange Golf Club. Its verandah is among the finest examples of decorative ironwork which survive in this country from the Victorian period.

BALMAIN, SYDNEY
This old stone house at Balmain has seen better days. Many fine old buildings fell into disrepair in the war and depression years because government-controlled rentals were so low that owners could not afford to spend money on repair work. Particularly during the depression years of the 1930s, large old homes and smaller terrace houses in the inner suburbs were tenanted by two or more families and sections of verandahs were often closed in like this to make an additional kitchen or bedroom. The rent-control laws have persisted since then to protect old-age tenants though in many cases this has been to the detriment of old-age buildings. But in inner-city suburbs such as Balmain and Paddington in Sydney and Carlton in Melbourne, old buildings like this one are being restored by new owners who appreciate the inherent charm which lies beneath a decrepit surface.

"DUNTRYLEAGUE",
ORANGE, NEW SOUTH WALES

93

KALGOORLIE, WESTERN AUSTRALIA

STROUD, NEW SOUTH WALES

KALGOORLIE, WESTERN AUSTRALIA
The proud character of a building can be entirely destroyed by the kind of architectural vandalism wrought on one half of the verandah of this house.

STROUD, NEW SOUTH WALES
The people of Stroud are justifiably proud of their fine post office which has been maintained in good condition. The decorative frieze panels of timber boarding have an interesting cut-out pattern.

HUNTERS HILL, SYDNEY
A delightful little stone cottage at Hunters Hill with a decorative verandah frieze pattern cut out of timber.

HUNTERS HILL, SYDNEY

MUDGEE, NEW SOUTH WALES

MUDGEE, NEW SOUTH WALES
The shabby reddish-brown of the old
shearers' slab hut on the historic
"Claralar" station gives it a rustic charm.

LANCER BARRACKS, PARRAMATTA,
NEW SOUTH WALES
The oldest continuously used military
establishment in Australia. The original
buildings were designed by John Watts
in 1816. The verandah of the two storey
section with its cast iron balustrade seen
in the foreground was added later. The
barracks are now the home of the Royal
New South Wales Lancers.

LANCER BARRACKS,
PARRAMATTA,
NEW SOUTH WALES

BLIGH HOUSE, SYDNEY

BLIGH HOUSE, SYDNEY
Built about 1836 for Robert Campbell,
this is the only remaining Georgian
town house within the city area of
Sydney. It is now occupied by the Royal
Australian College of General
Practitioners who, with the architect
Morton Herman, restored it in 1968. Its
simple Georgian facade has a verandah
supported by Greek Doric columns.

PADDINGTON, SYDNEY
The terrace housing of the inner-city
suburb of Paddington appealed to
migrants from Southern Europe who
were not afraid to paint their houses in
bright colours.

HUNTERS HILL, SYDNEY
Another Jules Joubert classic
sandstone house with its elegant cast
iron verandah decoration. The Joubert
brothers, Jules and Didier, and another
Frenchman, Charles Jeanneret, built
many sandstone houses on this harbour
peninsula and imported Italian
tradesmen to work the stone. Most of
Hunters Hill's best houses were built in
the four decades between 1850 and
1890. What a great repository of our
national heritage is held within the
bounds of this Sydney suburb.

PADDINGTON, SYDNEY

HUNTERS HILL, SYDNEY

ADELAIDE, SOUTH AUSTRALIA
Two superb old verandah buildings which have recently been restored. Both originally built as hotels, the red building is now a bank. The brown building is a hotel and restaurant and has an excellent verandah of robust character. The choice of colour harmonizes beautifully with the bluestone walls.

"FAIRFIELD", RICHMOND, NEW SOUTH WALES
This historic house has verandah ironwork of great delicacy. The main verandah is supported on iron posts and the cantilevered balcony by iron brackets.

CAMDEN, NEW SOUTH WALES
The Commercial Banking Company of Sydney's bank at Camden was built in 1877 and designed by G. A. Mansfield, doyen of bank architects of the late Victorian period in New South Wales. It has excellent ironwork on its verandahs.

ADELAIDE, SOUTH AUSTRALIA

"FAIRFIELD", RICHMOND, NEW SOUTH WALES

CAMDEN, NEW SOUTH WALES

KANIMBLA VALLEY, NEW SOUTH WALES

PADDINGTON, SYDNEY
Paddington is an inner-city suburb,
most of which was built in the forty
years between 1850 and 1890, in the
Victorian style. This building in
Gurner Street, before it was restored,
had an accumulation of many years of
advertising signs which made it
interesting in its own way but
camouflaged the beauty of its
architecture.

KANIMBLA VALLEY, NEW SOUTH
WALES
Early home of the pioneer O'Reilly
family near Hampden in the Kanimbla
Valley, built from timber slabs. Bernard
O'Reilly, the great bushman of
Lamington National Park, Queensland,
was born here.

PARKES, NEW SOUTH WALES
This old pisé house with its walls of
rammed mud covered with stucco has
stood for almost a hundred years. The
verandah roof shades the walls from the
rain and has helped keep them in
excellent condition.

PADDINGTON, SYDNEY

PARKES, NEW SOUTH WALES

KINGS CROSS, SYDNEY

BUNDABERG, QUEENSLAND

KINGS CROSS, SYDNEY
It is very uncommon to find terrace houses in Australia which are four storeys high. The ornate ironwork of this row in Roslyn Gardens is in need of restoration.

BUNDABERG, QUEENSLAND
Bundaberg is a noteworthy city of fine pubs with large verandahs. A good cool place to drink is on the top verandah overlooking the city streets, yet few hotels make use of their verandahs for out-of-doors drinking.

BROOME, WESTERN AUSTRALIA
The old courthouse of Broome is a simple building which is given a certain dignity by the high roof which slopes down to form a verandah all round. Not only does it shade the walls from the hot sun but it also gives shelter from the heavy rain of the monsoon season, when the hot humid weather makes it necessary to have doors and windows wide open for plenty of ventilation.

BROOME,
WESTERN AUSTRALIA

CUE, WESTERN AUSTRALIA

BOULDER, WESTERN AUSTRALIA

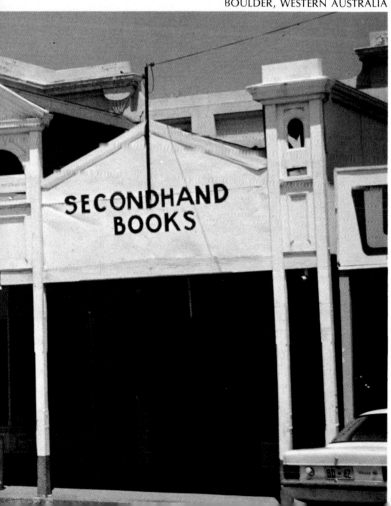

SECONDHAND
BOOKS

CUE, WESTERN AUSTRALIA
Another old frontier mining town, now
virtually a ghost town. Many stone
buildings are found in areas such as this
which have little good building timber.
This building evokes the rugged
hardship of the early mining days.

BOULDER, WESTERN AUSTRALIA
Boulder, with its sister city Kalgoorlie, is
a wealthy gold mining centre. Most of
the town was built after 1880. The
idiosyncratic style of this verandah is an
example of the surprises one can find in
old frontier towns.

HUNTERS HILL, SYDNEY
This verandah with its bull-nosed iron
and cast iron lace looks out over the
Lane Cove River.

BRISBANE, QUEENSLAND

Sadly, the wonderful verandahs of the famous Bellevue Hotel no longer exist. It stood next to Parliament House and one can imagine the very close link which existed over the years between these two important chambers. It was a popular place for Parliamentarians to stay while the House was in session and it is intriguing to wonder how many important decisions of affairs of State were made over a cold glass of Four-X beer on its cool verandah. The destruction of this building of such grace and well-being is a folly without parallel. As cities destroy their links with the past they destroy their very souls and all in the cause of "progress".

PORT PIRIE, SOUTH AUSTRALIA
It would take little work to restore these
verandahs to a good state of repair.
Their value is immense, not only in
terms of the shelter they give the
footpath but also for the unique
character they give to the streetscape.

**POST OFFICE, CAMPBELLTOWN, NEW
SOUTH WALES**
Campbelltown was one of the first
seven country postal depots in New
South Wales. The first postmaster, John
Scarr, was appointed in 1828. The
present building was designed by James
Barnet, built in 1881, and is an example
of his Italianate style of country post
offices. The clock and upper storey
verandah were added in 1883 by the
local architect, A. R. Payton.

LYNTON, WESTERN AUSTRALIA
The Commandant's residence of the
old convict hiring station at Lynton,
with its extensive verandahs, is an
important historic building in urgent
need of restoration.

PORT PIRIE, SOUTH AUSTRALIA

POST OFFICE,
CAMPBELLTOWN,
NEW SOUTH WALES

LYNTON, WESTERN AUSTRALIA

COOGEE, SYDNEY
A simple verandah adds dignity to this
fine old sandstone home at Coogee.

GRENFELL, NEW SOUTH WALES
Grenfell still retains many of its street verandahs. It was here that poet Henry Lawson was born in 1867 and his mother would have carried him beneath these same verandahs.

ALBURY, NEW SOUTH WALES
An old inn near Albury, built about 1865, is now a private home. Founded in 1824, Albury on the Murray River developed slowly until the 1850s. It is now a thriving city.

GLEBE, SYDNEY
Architecture of a century ago rusting and decaying but inherently beautiful. Glebe in the 1870s was one of Sydney's most fashionable suburbs. It later became a slum but is now being restored as an important area of Victorian architecture.

BOULDER, WESTERN AUSTRALIA
The city of Boulder near Kalgoorlie is amongst Australia's best in terms of its wealth of remaining street verandahs.

GRENFELL, NEW SOUTH WALES

ALBURY, NEW SOUTH WALES

GLEBE, SYDNEY

BOULDER, WESTERN AUSTRALIA

DORRIGO, NEW SOUTH WALES

COOKTOWN, QUEENSLAND

DORRIGO, NEW SOUTH WALES
Dorrigo developed as an important timber-getting town and much of the State's cedar came from this area.

KALUMBURU, WESTERN AUSTRALIA
An early Spanish Roman Catholic mission built of local stone, its gable ends show a distinct Spanish influence. Its narrow iron verandah shelters the walls from the hot sun.

COOKTOWN, QUEENSLAND
The famous old Bank of New South Wales with its wide verandah overlooks the once thriving settlement of Cooktown on Cape York Peninsula.

KALUMBURU,
WESTERN AUSTRALIA

GARDEN ISLAND, SYDNEY

The old barracks at Garden Island, the naval establishment in Sydney Harbour, was designed by James Barnet and built in 1887. The verandah structure is of iron with iron balustrades. Garden Island is now completely joined to the mainland by the construction of the naval dockyard.

DUBBO, NEW SOUTH WALES

This stone house with its verandah ornately decorated with cast iron "lace" is now used by the N.S.W. Public Transport Commission as a railway engineer's office.

PATERSON, NEW SOUTH WALES

An early cottage at Paterson in the Hunter Valley is built of split slabs of local hardwood placed side by side, with the joints caulked. The bull-nosed shape of the galvanized iron verandah roof was popular in the 1860s when this cottage was built.

DUBBO, NEW SOUTH WALES

This former bank building is now the Dubbo Museum. The verandah is supported by cast iron Greek Ionic columns. It is an excellent example of bank architecture of the Victorian period but when it was no longer considered useful it was intended for demolition. Only the swift action of the citizens of Dubbo and the then mayor, the late Alderman Ford, saved it. Many western country towns have fine examples of early Australian architecture and their loss would impoverish the towns not only in their heritage but also in the financial benefits of their tourist income.

GARDEN ISLAND, SYDNEY

DUBBO, NEW SOUTH WALES

PATERSON, NEW SOUTH WALES

DUBBO, NEW SOUTH WALES

HUNTERS HILL, SYDNEY

ADELAIDE, SOUTH AUSTRALIA

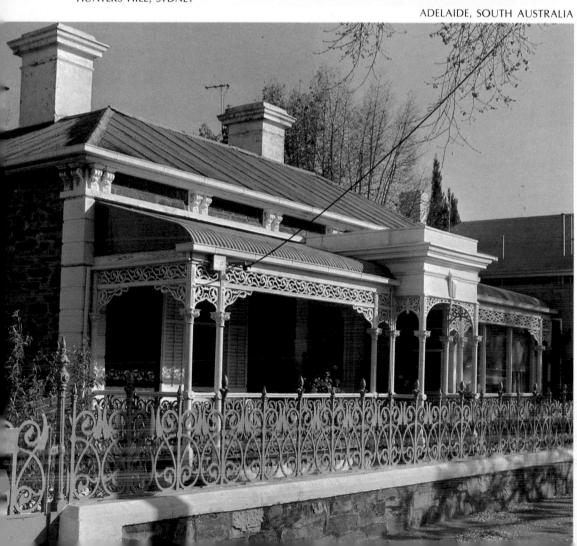

"ROSENEATH", PARRAMATTA, NEW SOUTH WALES

HUNTERS HILL, SYDNEY
Another of the Hunters Hill houses built by the Joubert brothers, this one has an interesting pattern in its timber verandah balustrade.

ADELAIDE, SOUTH AUSTRALIA
Local bluestone is a very common building material in Adelaide. Its warm dark colour contrasts well with the white ironwork of the verandah, a combination characteristic of houses of this period in the area. The front fence is a superb piece of old wrought iron work.

"ROSENEATH", PARRAMATTA, NEW SOUTH WALES
This Colonial Georgian house with its simple verandah supported by turned timber columns was built in 1837. The verandah and house are both covered by the one roof and the verandah extends around three sides of the house. Roseneath is notable for its excellent proportions.

CHATSWOOD, SYDNEY
Brick is a very plentiful building material in Sydney because of unlimited deposits of good brickmaking shale and clay. The verandah roof on this Victorian style house in Chatswood, a northern suburb of Sydney, has a slight curve in the galvanized iron sheeting.

CHATSWOOD, SYDNEY

121

"THROSBY PARK", MOSS VALE, NEW SOUTH WALES

Built by Charles Throsby in 1834, the house has a stone flagged verandah on three sides. Throsby Park has remained in the ownership of the original family ever since.

PADDINGTON, SYDNEY

A corner shop in historic Paddington has been converted into a restaurant. The delicate beauty of the cast iron "lace" on its balcony is well shown in silhouette against the floodlit walls. Australia during the Victorian period developed the use of decorative cast iron in a unique and beautiful way and to an extent which can only be paralleled by a few other places such as New Orleans in the U.S.A.

PADDINGTON, SYDNEY

PADDINGTON, SYDNEY
The corner balcony of the famous
Hungry Horse Restaurant in Paddington
is a superb example of its kind.

The traditional squatter's chair was
once a common piece of verandah
furniture but not many are seen these
days.

"LOCKYERSLEIGH", GOULBURN, NEW SOUTH WALES

The original floor of this country homestead was built in the late 1820s in simple Georgian style with stone verandah columns. The original owner, Major Edmund Lockyer, suffered financial difficulties in the depression of the 1840s and in 1855 he sold the property. Shortly afterwards the upper storey was added in the style of the early Victorian period with balustrade and columns of filigree cast iron

CASSILIS, NEW SOUTH WALES

The homestead verandah of the country property of Douglass Baglin is well-used as a place to sit in the shade and relax with a cool drink.

BRISBANE, QUEENSLAND

Without its spacious verandah this timber building in Brisbane would lose its grace and utility.

BACK PAGE
GULGONG

These buildings in Gulgong have recently been restored and add their own character and charm to the streetscape of a historic town.

"LOCKYERSLEIGH",
GOULBURN,
NEW SOUTH WALES

CASSILIS, NEW SOUTH WALES

BRISBANE, QUEENSLAND

GULGONG